PETERBOROUGH
THEN & NOW

IN COLOUR

JUNE & VERNON BULL

The History Press

First published in 2013

The History Press
The Mill, Brimscombe Port
Stroud, Gloucestershire, GL5 2QG
www.thehistorypress.co.uk

British Library Cataloguing in Publication Data.
A catalogue record for this book is available from the British Library.

ISBN 978 0 7524 8147 0

Typesetting and origination by The History Press
Printed in India.

CONTENTS

ACKNOWLEDGEMENTS

In compiling the content for this book we sought to ensure that the text content is factually correct to the best of our knowledge, enthralling and stimulating. The authors are indebted to the following people; we could not have done it without them: the late Messrs Harry Miles; John Jack Gaunt; Harry Hurst; and Stanley Hoare; and Mrs Josephine Gillatt. Special thanks go to: Stephen Perry; Gwen Hurst; John Gillatt; Jean Miles; and John & Vera Seeley.

INTRODUCTION

Peterborough has a rich history and heritage which tells a gripping story. Whether Peterborough is your home, or you live nearby, or you are simply visiting then this book explores the city in lots of different ways.

It takes us through a pageant of progress from Monastic times to the present day and traces some of the various ways in which the hamlet has grown into the city it is today. We see how the town has developed over the centuries and how today's successes have their roots in yesteryear.

Through the matching of old images with modern ones – taken from the same camera location today – the book allows the reader to soak in the many changes that have occurred over the intervening years.

These ninety images trace some of the most significant aspects of the city. It is our involvement with the local history society which has enabled us to work with such enthusiasm on this project. We trust this book provides as much pleasure for the reader as it did for us in compiling it. We hope it invokes many happy memories for older residents, as well as offering a deeper insight to new residents and to those that come to work in the city, or are visiting it for the first time.

June & Vernon Bull, 2013

GUILDHALL AND MARKET PLACE

THE MARKET CROSS or Guildhall building was partly or completely rebuilt by John Lovin in 1671. It was adorned with the city's coat of arms and later a clock, and a room was erected over the old piazza. Previously, there was a single-storey market cross on this site from at least 1613. The cost of erecting the 1671 building was defrayed partly by public subscription, partly by a donation from Lord Fitzwilliam, who controlled the local Parliamentary elections, and finally by an issue of specially struck Peterborough halfpence coins. When Peterborough was incorporated (i.e. given city status) in 1874, the Guildhall was used as a council chamber.

In 1930, new municipal buildings were erected in Bridge Street and meetings in the Guildhall were discontinued. The new town hall in Bridge Street was officially opened by Alderman Whitsted on 16 October 1933. The Guildhall was scheduled as an ancient monument in 1928 when it was completely restored by the city corporation under the advice of the Society for the Preservation of Ancient Buildings.

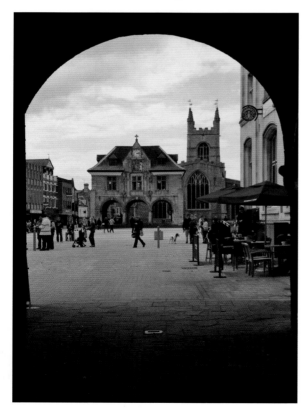

In 1957 Peterborough became twinned with Bourges in France. A plaque depicting the Bourges coat of arms can be seen on the east side of the Guildhall. Today the upper room is unused but the open space below provides a venue for civic, art and cultural events. Market stalls use to be located around the fountain, which was erected as a memorial to the first mayor of the city, Henry Pearson Gates. He held this position on four separate occasions. The memorial was unveiled on 14 June 1898 and was a gift from Mrs Gates. In 1967 it was moved to Bishops Road Gardens without its water basins. In 1963 the market moved from here to its present site – the area bounded by Northminster and accessed via Laxton Square, Cattle Market Road and Market Way. It was in this year that the Market Place was renamed Cathedral Square.

THE CORN EXCHANGE

THE PETERBOROUGH CORN Exchange Co. was formed on
23 December 1847 at the Angel Hotel in Narrow Bridge
Street. The Corn Exchange was built on the site of the Patent
Theatre, which stood on the western portion fronting Butchers
Row – roughly where Kings Street to St John's Square is today.
Theatre experienced a revival in England with the restoration
of King Charles II, giving the performing arts a new lease of
life. In Peterborough, at the close of the eighteenth century, a
small syndicate of local clergy and other gentlemen funded the
building of the Patent Theatre.

It is believed that earlier theatres existed on the site and
records show that in 1811 the local playhouse proprietors
included the Revd Henry Freeman of Alwalton, the Revd
Robert Roberts of Stoke Doyle, Lord Fitzwilliam, and Messrs
William Squire and Wright Thomas Squire – merchant
bankers and founders of Squires Bank, Peterborough. The site
of the Corn Exchange building was bought for £525 by the
Peterborough Corn Exchange Co. It was officially opened on

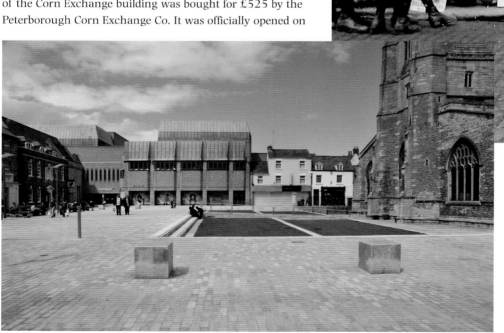

30 September 1848 and housed ninety-four stands – selling all manner of wheat, corn, barley, grain and other local agricultural produce.

The Corn Exchange building was enlarged several times, and a new roof was added in 1912. The directors in 1922 (at the time of this postcard) were George Crick (chairman), William Buckle (secretary), Charles Crick, William Beaver, Arthur Bird, and William Moore. The market was held each Saturday and opening times were from 12.00 p.m. to 3.30 p.m. for the sale of corn, potatoes and other agricultural commodities. At other times it was used for social events and auction sales. The Corn Exchange closed in 1962 and was demolished in June 1964 to make way for the Norwich Union Building. The latter building was demolished in November 2009 to make way for St John's Square, which was completed in 2011.

LONG CAUSEWAY

FROM ANGLO-SAXON times up until the mid-sixteenth century, the control of the town and its roads came under the authority of the various abbots who, in turn, came under the watchful eye of the Bishop of Lincoln (at that time Peterborough fell under the diocese of Lincoln). In those days, the construction of roads and streets was of a very poor standard and pedestrian access was often impossible. These roads and streets were perpetually damaged due to carts, and the hooves of cattle, sheep and horses. The solution for pedestrians was resolved by walkways or 'causeways'.

A prime example is Long Causeway, which was laid from the Marketstede (Market Place/ Cathedral Square) to Westgate. There was a ditch, or moat, dug next to the monastery's

west wall and the material taken up was placed to the side so that people could walk along the top of it. Excavations in the Victorian period led to the discovery of other streets which had a raised ridge on one side of the road, ranging between 15–18in higher than the level of the road. The top layer was cobbles but underneath there were layers of bones and small shells. In the left forefront of the 1962 postcard is R.J. Glass Ltd (No. 1–5) – this shop sold curtains, millinery and ladies' clothes. On the immediate right (east side) one can just see the Double Diamond sign, hanging outside Paten & Co. Ltd wine merchants, and further down, at No. 32, was the Bird in Hand pub.

Long Causeway as a main road links the Market Place (renamed Cathedral Square in 1963) to the junction of Westgate, Broadway and Midgate. It was part of the A15 and the A47 routes. Today the whole area is pedestrianised and shoppers can enjoy a more casual and sedate approach to their activities.

NARROW BRIDGE STREET

THE 1880 SKETCH (*opposite*) shows how constricted the road was before it was widened (it was only 33ft at its widest point). Prior to 1773 Narrow Street, which took in the section from the Market Place to Albert Place, was known as Hithegate. Broad Bridge Street took in the southern section of Bridge Street from the junction of Bishops Road and Albert Place to the River Nene. On the sketch one can see Paviour's clock protruding from a building on the left. It was built by Mr Whatley Paviour, who ran a watchmaker's shop in Narrow Street. In the 1898 view

you can see George Caster, the printer and stationer's shop in Market Place, next to the Cathedral gateway in the far background. Next door was the London Clothing Co., and the shop with awnings is the wine and spirit merchants – Nichols & Co. Ltd. These premises in Market Place were demolished in 1929 to make way for the widening of Narrow Bridge Street.

In the immediate right foreground of the 1898 view is J.H. Pearson, the chemist, at No. 1 Narrow Street. The demolition of this

property along with all the buildings on the east side, plus part of the Cathedral's Palace Gardens, helped make the Bridge Street we know today.

It was the expansion of the city boundaries in 1929 which brought an urgent need for more municipal office space. The City Council in 1904 had bought land between Midgate and the Cattle Market with the intention of building a town hall and offices on the Long Causeway and Midgate corner. By 1920 this project was deemed inadequate and it was proposed to widen Narrow Bridge Street and to construct a new bridge over the river to replace the existing iron structure (built in 1872) – considered too narrow and unsafe.

In 1929 the mayor's casting vote decided that the widening of Narrow Bridge Street should go ahead. Later that year the first sod was turned by the mayor, Alderman Arthur Craig. The foundation stone of the existing town hall was laid by Prince George, Duke of Kent, on 28 June 1929.

PARK ROAD

HERE IS THE town end of Park Road with the Baptist Chapel (Barrass Memorial Hall) in the immediate right foreground. The Park Road church was officially opened by the pastor's wife, Mrs Knee, on 11 April 1907. The Barrass Memorial Hall adjoining it was built on 26 May 1904 as a memorial to the Revd Thomas Barrass, for many years a minister of the church. Park Road Baptist Chapel underwent major reconstruction in 1988. Further down on the right-hand side is the Co-operative Society hall with shops underneath. The Peterborough and District Co-operative Society Ltd was established in 1876 with its registered offices at the Central Stores, Park Road. The 30th annual Co-operative Congress was held in Peterborough from 30 May to 1 June 1898. The Peterborough Society's

general manager at this time was Mr William Parrott who had twenty-one years of continuous service under his belt.

The top part of Park Road (from Westgate to Geneva Street) was constructed in the 1870s and was for a long time known as Houghton Street. On the left-hand side is Ellis Bell, tailor and outfitter, located at No. 20–22 Park Road; further down on the left towards Westgate is the sign for the offices of Northants Brewery Co. Ltd at No. 16 Park Road.

Today the Co-operative store is owned by Beales – a Bournemouth-based company who signed a deal worth an initial £7.5 million in 2011 to buy nineteen stores from Anglia Regional Co-operative Society, including this store on the corner of Westgate and Park Road. This made Beales the third largest department store chain in the UK, doubling its workforce to 2,500.

No. 57 WESTGATE

HERE IS THE new child's bicycle saddle which fixed to the crossbar and cost 3s to buy from F. & G.W. Burrows' shop at No. 57 Westgate, next to the Crown Inn on Westgate. Burrows were cycle and motor cycle dealers who also had a garage in Dogsthorpe Road.

   Today the Tom Thumb is best known for making horse bits. Cycling was a very popular pastime at the turn of the last century and Peterborough had its fair share of cycling clubs.
The Peterborough Cycling Club was established in 1874 and was affiliated to the National Cyclists' Union. In 1924 the club celebrated its fiftieth year by election to life membership of Mr E. Adams, Mr W. Cheavin, Mr W. Bath, Messrs R. & G. Julyan, Mr G. Neale, Mr W. Rimes, Mr W. Tombs,

THE NEW

"Tom Thumb"

SADDLE Co.,

57, Westgate,

PETERBORO'.

Order a Sample.
Retails at 3/-
It's a Money
    . . Maker.
A Good Margin
   for Agents.

Obtainable of all
Factors and Cycle
Stores throughout
   the World.

Mr E. Thompson, Mr G. Keeble and Mr A. Roberston. The latter was Arthur 'Archie' Roberston who was a 1908 Olympian winning gold and silver medals in athletics. At the age of thirty, after a track and cross-country career lasting four years, Archie returned to cycling. All his brothers were keen cyclists; and his younger brother Dubs Robertson competed in the London 1908 Olympic Games, held at White City – coming seventh in the finals of the 100km cycling event.

Westgate originally connected St Leonard's Street to the junction of Long Causeway, Broadway and Midgate and used to be named Webstergate – meaning road of weavers. The present-day shop site now forms part of the Queensgate shopping centre (John Lewis' office entrance).

Cycling was a very popular pastime and remains so today – especially as a competitive sport. Indeed, it's heartening that the city has hosted the Halfords Tour Series over the last four years and hopes to do so again in May 2013. Peterborough is only one of three venues to have hosted the Tour Series rounds in every season of this team-based series.

NARROW BRIDGE STREET

THIS SHOPFRONT, WITH an impressive row of staff on parade, shows that Lipton's sold not only tea but biscuits, cocoa, chocolate, confectionery, pickles, sauces, jams and jellies, marmalade, sausages, potted meats, coffee essence, cornflour, toffees, farinaceous (starch) preparations and all manner of provisions. It looks as though the full complement of staff is standing proud outside of No. 52 Narrow Street on this real picture postcard.

Lipton stores were founded by Thomas Johnstone Lipton in Glasgow. He expanded quickly and eventually he had a chain of shops across Scotland and later throughout Britain. By 1888 he had 300 stores. A decade later, in 1898, Lipton yielded to the public demand and allowed his empire to become a limited company, and on 2 June 1898 he directed his first shareholders meeting. The clamour for shares was incredible; the professionals had failed to take account of the regard and affection that the public had for the Lipton brand. His goods were given the royal seal of approval not only by King George V but also the King of Spain and the King and Queen of Italy.

Today the shop site is occupied by bonmarché – a ladies fashionware outlet owned by J.D. Williams. The present-day view was taken on 2 June 2012 – the first day of the official long weekend of the Queen's Diamond Jubilee celebrations.

Some shops in Bridge Street were affected as the focus of retail trading turned to Queensgate Shopping Centre which opened in 1982 with over ninety indoor stores. More recently, a number of retailers in Bridge Street have had to close because of the current economic downturn with apparently some of the smaller independent outlets being more acutely affected.

No. 27 VERGETTE STREET

STANDING PROUD OUTSIDE his shop is owner Charles Hammond, along with an assortment of meat and foul. Hammond only traded here for a short while, as in the 1890 directory of trades he was listed as a beer retailer and butcher at No. 175 Cromwell Road, along with a Joseph Hammond. In 1898 George Markham was the butcher at No. 27 Vergette Street followed by Charles Hammond, and then some fifteen years later the butchers at No. 27 Vergette Street was run by Alfred Hand. Certainly today the hygiene inspectors would have a field day with these cuts of meat attracting flies and all sorts in the heat! Vergette Street was so named because of the Vergette family who ran many local businesses and shops, the most notable being

William Vergette, a wholesale grocer, Edward Vergette who was mayor in 1885 and Charles Vergette who was mayor in 1919. The name Vergette is synonymous with the well-known Peterborough firm of Fox & Vergette – auctioneers and valuers – established in 1802. The firm was originally founded by Mr John Fox snr in Huntingdon, and he was followed by his son, John, who came to Peterborough some years after. In 1884 John Fox jnr was joined by Mr Samuel Vergette, and in 1888 Mr Charles Vergette also joined the firm.

The firm moved offices from Narrow Street, opposite the Angel Hotel, to Priestgate in 1923. They changed their name to Fox Vergette & Richardsons in January 1973, and shortened it to Vergettes from 2 June 1977. They remained in Priestgate until 1980. Today, the butchers shop at No. 27 Vergette Street is a residential property.

21

EMBASSY THEATRE

WORK STARTED ON the building of the Embassy Theatre in Broadway on 26 January 1937. On Monday 1 November 1937 the Embassy officially opened to the public. The owner Jack Bancroft received a multitude of cheers for all he had achieved in having this

Art Deco theatre built in the city centre, which was the highest building after the cathedral. It was constructed of 1 million local Fletton bricks; there were 196 windows and 250 doors. It took 2,000 yards of Wilton carpet and the lower foyer had under-floor heating beneath Italian marble tiles. Mr H. Hall (formerly the personal touring manager of Gracie Fields) was appointed manager. The Embassy Theatre was designed by David Nye with a seating capacity of 1,484. Various artists such as George Formby, Laurel and Hardy, and Ivor Novello appeared at the theatre. In 1965 the Associated British Cinemas acquired the Embassy but kept its name until it became the ABC cinema. It closed as a single-screen cinema on 24 January 1981 and reopened as a triple-screen cinema on 14 May 1981.

A year or two after this the main cinema was again used as a stage. The ABC then became the Cannon Cinema which in turn closed in 1989. Nowadays the building is used as a plush nightspot – Edward's Bar – which holds karaoke nights and has a regular DJ, as well as plasma screens, a small dance floor, and seating for 1,000 people.

KINGS STREET

THE CITADEL, ERECTED in 1891, was in Kings Street, which originally linked Cowgate to Queen Street, but today it is a cul-de-sac off Cowgate. It could hold up to 700 people. Weekly services were held on Sundays, with a prayer meeting at 7 a.m., holiness at 11 a.m., testimony at 3 p.m. and salvation at 6.30 p.m. The Citadel was open for other various events and services on weekdays. In 1927 the Senior Salvation Army Band was under the leadership of Bandmaster Tom Gibbs. The Salvation Army also owned the Pipe Lane Mission Hall in Eastgate and used it as an education centre. It is significant that the Peterborough Citadel opened in 1891 as the movement's founder, William Booth, publically signed 'Darkest England' (now the Salvation Army's Social Work Trust Deed) on 30 January 1891.

Today the Peterborough Salvation Army Citadel has its base at No. 1203 Bourges Boulevard where it continues to extend a helping hand to those who are homeless, friendless and in need. In 1888 Captain Margaret Berry formed the first senior Salvation Army

Band in Peterborough, under the leadership of Bandmaster Reuben Dennis. It is nearly 125 years later and the band has had thirteen different leaders and has toured the UK extensively.

Presently the band has a membership of around forty with an average age of sixty-three. One of the Salvationists' biggest admirers and well-known local personalities was James Blades OBE (1901–1999) – a percussionist. He was born at No. 6 Albert Place and lived with his parents, grandparents, a cousin and three brothers. From a very early age he fell in love with drumming after watching a member of the local Salvation Army Band banging a bass drum.

In 1935 he created the sound of the gong at the beginning of movies made by J. Arthur Rank studios. James' recording was mimed by boxer William Thomas Wells (better known as Bombardier Billy Wells). The most notable sound James made was the dot-dot-dot-dash ditty of 'V for Victory' Morse code that the BBC broadcast to encourage the Resistance in continental Europe during the Second World War.

Today the site of the Kings Street Citadel appears to be undergoing a makeover. Scaffolding can be seen outside of the relatively modern offices and part of the Queensgate Shopping Centre can be seen in the left background.

CHURCH STREET

LOOKING EAST TOWARDS Market Place (now Cathedral Square) this view of the 1911 Coronation procession includes a steam tractor pulling a float with a crown and Union Jack made of leather. The float won first prize with its apt slogan 'Nothing Like Leather'.

This shot takes in the south porch of Peterborough parish church, St John the Baptist, built between 1402 and 1407. Municipal offices adjoin the Guildhall which at this time was the town hall. Adjacent to the float can be seen the hut used by taxi and carriage drivers. At one time the entire road was Cowgate, and in the first half of the nineteenth century it was named Church Street. King George V came to the throne on the death of his father Edward VII on the 6 May 1910.

Today's view is very different. The council offices (later a police post) next to the Guildhall have been demolished and the church railings pictured on the south side of St John's were

removed in 2010 along with the trees and bushes. Church Street is now largely pedestrianised and the taxi rank was relocated some sixty years ago. The west side of the seventeenth-century Guildhall, along with the west end of the early fifteenth-century St John the Baptist church – Peterborough parish church – are now more visible and accessible, making the landscape more welcoming, and highlighting both these historic gems in the heart of the city centre.

The much-debated fountains in Cathedral Square were unveiled in June 2010. The Square has no road kerbs, forming a wall-to-wall stone mat. Two triangular groups of in-ground, highly controllable water jets shape a diagonal pedestrian route.

The redevelopment of the city centre and the making of St John's Square formed part of the city's Public Realm Strategy costing £12.6 million.

LINCOLN ROAD

HERE WE SEE a wonderfully animated Lincoln Road with a tram on its way from Long Causeway to either Dogsthorpe or Walton. On the left is a horse-drawn baker's van and on the right is a horse and carriage with a groom standing nearby. A bicycle can be seen propped up against the lamppost adjacent to the horse and carriage and to complete the array of movement and various forms of transport – pedestrians can be seen on both sides of the road.

The turning on the immediate right is to Lincoln Road East (renamed Burghley Road from 1956). This road links Lincoln Road to Park Road and was named after the 6th Marquess

of Exeter, David George Brownlow Cecil – styled Lord Burghley before 1956. David Burghley was a Conservative politician and athlete. He won the gold medal in 1928 for the 400m hurdles at the Olympic Games in Amsterdam.

In 1931 he was elected as Member of Parliament for Peterborough until he was defeated in 1943 by Viscount Suirdale (kidnapped, along with his wife, by the IRA in June 1974 and released after a week).

Today the junction of Lincoln Road and Burghley Road is a roundabout and traffic flow is quite congested at peak times.

The mainly Victorian and Edwardian homes have been made into flats or bedsits and very few today retain their original single-family occupancy. Some of the properties have been made into commercial premises like shops or hotels.

Trams disappeared in 1930 when buses and cars became more popular. The cobbled road at the junction of Lincoln Road and Lincoln Road East (now Burghley Road) has long-since been tarmacked over. Lincoln Road used to form part of the A15 trunk road, so named because of the destination the road eventually reaches.

DOGSTHORPE ROAD

THIS IS QUITE a rare postcard showing Princes Street turning in the right foreground. Princes Street then becomes Princes Gate with its proximity to the city's central park and then as a continuum becomes Princes Gardens which takes you onto Eastfield Road. Dogsthorpe was once a hamlet in the township of Peterborough and the curiosity of this parish – Dogsthorpe with Garton End – is that parts of it in 1927 dipped into Peterborough Park Crescent. Several prominent citizens have lived here, such as Major John Shipley Ellis of Abbeyfields, Park Crescent; the solicitor Reginald Norris, Park Crescent; and the engineer John Perkins, Park Crescent.

Main buildings in Dogsthorpe village during the time of this postcard include: Dogsthorpe Grange, occupied at this time by the Misses Kate and Margaret Craig; Manor Farm occupied by Mr James Godfrey; the Blue Bell Inn – publican Mr Charles Goodyear; The Cedars, occupied by Emily Higgins; Lawn House, occupied by the farmer Mr Frank Odam; The Laurels, occupied

by Leonard Letch; the confectioner Mr Herbert Neaverson lived at Airedale House; and William Willson, a pig-powder manufacturer, lived at the Manor House.

The Laurels stood next to the Blue Bell Inn but was demolished to make way for the existing flats. The largest building in Dogsthorpe was The Grange which had fifteen rooms. The next most substantial property in Dogsthorpe was Lawn House, which had nine rooms.

Other notable people included Walter Thompson of Woodbyth in Dogsthorpe Road – part of John Thompson & Sons Ltd ecclesiastical contractors etc. Dogsthorpe's sub-postmaster in 1927 was Mr J. Sharpe and the parish church was Paston. Its district councillor at this time was Brigadier-General William Strong of Thorpe Hall, Longthorpe. Dogsthorpe School was built in 1876 and enlarged in 1896 – it accommodated 140 pupils. The school master in 1927 was Mr Robert Baker. Interestingly, in this vintage postcard the building with the prominent pitched roof in the right foreground was the forerunner to All Saints School.

Today's view of Dogsthorpe Road shows the shop on the corner as a general store; the tramlines disappeared over eighty years ago. Otherwise, the street remains predominantly residential.

No. 94 DOGSTHORPE ROAD

THIS REAL PHOTOGRAPHIC postcard shows Reuben Bingham (general dealer and greengrocer) returning home from market outside the Co-operative stores and butchers at the corner of Dogsthorpe Road and All Saints Road. The latter links Dogsthorpe Road to Park Road.

When Reuben retired, the shop was taken over by his son Reuben Kenneth Bingham. In 1927 Reuben Bingham lived at No. 133 Dogsthorpe Road.

Running a shop in the early twentieth century meant long hours but shops, markets and shopping were important to the people of Peterborough, just as they had been in Victorian times. Shops and shopping brought commercial prosperity to the locality and

gave local people the opportunity to buy a wide range of goods as society became more and more consumer-orientated.

The transition from the nineteenth to the twentieth century saw a gradual reduction in the number of family-owned shops in the city, as national retail firms arrived, such as Liptons, Maypole Dairies and other household names including the Co-op. The question of shop opening hours was regularly discussed in the early decades of the twentieth century – with some shops open from 6 a.m. until just before midnight. Shop assistants, many of whom lived above the shop, complained of long hours and poor pay. The Co-operative movement started in Peterborough in 1876 and the trading rules stated that the objects of the society are to carry on the business of a storekeeper, general dealer and universal provider in all its branches.

Today the former Co-operative shop on the corner of Dogsthorpe Road and All Saints Road is a European, Asian and Middle Eastern food store. All Saints Road was named after the church which is on the corner of Park Road and All Saints Road. The church was built in two phases – in 1886 and 1901 – and the architect was Temple Moore.

PADHOLME ROAD

THIS EDWARDIAN REAL photographic postcard shows people posing for the photographer on both sides of the road. Padholme Road is in Eastfield and at this time linked Eastfield Road to Storey's Bar Road. Previously it was called Boongate Road with the name Padholme being a derivative of the name of a field the road originally crossed; that field being called Padinholm.

This view looks towards Eastfield Road along the east side of Broadway Cemetery. The Broadway Cemetery was opened on 8 May 1858 and can be accessed on foot from Eastfield Road. The first burial was that of J.W. Bower. This cemetery eventually closed to new burials, but for those who had a right to burial in a family plot, internment continued until 1955.

From May 1919 onwards, the new cemetery on the corner of Newark Avenue and Eastfield Road was opened for standard earthen burials, brick-lined graves and cremated remains in plots or vaults.

From the turn of the last century, Messrs T.W. Mays Ltd ran a tallow (candles and soap) factory at Padholme Road, but this seems to have disappeared by 1940. This refinery was run from a wooden and brick shed and was probably sited more towards what is now Padholme Road East.

The Air Raid Precaution (ARP) depot was located at No. 61 Padholme Road during the Second World War. The main purpose of ARP wardens was to patrol the streets during blackouts to ensure that no light was visible. They also had the task of reporting any bomb damage and assessing the need for help from the emergency services and rescue services. They used their knowledge of their local areas to help find and reunite family members who had been separated in the rush to find shelters from bombs. Today the road remains largely residential.

PADHOLME ROAD

THIS POSTCARD SHOWS Cavendish Street junction on the immediate left, and a little further down on the right is the junction of Padholme Road and Charles Street. In this 1910 scene gas street lighting has arrived, while in the previous 1906 postcard the lampposts are wholly absent. Gas continued to be a form of street lighting up until electricity started to become popular, which started to be introduced wholesale in 1933. The gas lanterns were modified to take electric wiring and bulbs.

Cavendish Street is named after William Cavendish, one of the city's MPs from 1847 to 1852. He was also president of the Peterborough Agricultural Society. Cavendish Street was extended in 1935.

Charles Street is said to be named after George Charles Wentworth Fitzwilliam who appears to have lived a fairly modest life at Milton Hall.

Under his stewardship, the stately home was never extended nor did it undergo any major renovations.

During 1910 some of the principal occupants of Padholme Road included William Duddington, organist; G. & W.H. Burch, Rose Nurseries at No. 66–74 Padholme Road; and the blacksmith Mr James Phillips at No. 54 Padholme Road.

Today, the area is multi-ethnic with mixed-occupancy housing, including flats and bedsits, as many owner/occupiers have moved out and rented their premises to newcomers from many areas of the world.

Padholme Road is in East Ward for electoral purposes and was contested in the May 2012 local elections by June Bull (Conservative), Paul Furnborough (Green), Abid Hussain (Liberal Democrat) and Joanne Johnson (Labour). Johnson won her first election (gaining 265 votes more than the second placed Conservative candidate) to join her existing Labour colleague, Cllr Nabil Shabbir and the Conservative incumbent and former mayor, Cllr Marion Todd.

COWGATE

THE ORIGINAL GRAVEYARD of the old St John's church in Boongate was in St John's Close, on the south side of the cathedral. In 1803 it was full and the churchwardens bought 3 acres of farmland at the end of Cowgate, the first burial taking place in 1805.

At the turn of the twentieth century an approach road was made through the graveyard and eventually the graveyard was bought by the Peterborough Development Corporation to make way for the existing Crescent roundabout in the 1970s. Exhumed bodies were reinterred at the Eastfield (corner of Newark Avenue and Eastfield Road) Cemetery.

Apparently and spookily, this graveyard is said to be one of the last places in the UK to have been raided by gruesome bodysnatchers. Bodysnatching was common in the eighteenth and

early nineteenth century as doctors needed to practice on human corpses but it was illegal for them to do so, except on those of deceased criminals. This all changed with the Anatomy Act of 1832.

These men would dig up the corpses and sell them on to doctors. The first incident of bodysnatchers in Peterborough took place in November 1828 when one evening a cart was seen outside Cowgate Cemetery with two men loading suspicious sacks onto it. The alarm was raised and the men fled, with a cart chase ending near Norman Cross, outside Peterborough. It was here that the men abandoned their cart and fled over the fields. The next recorded bodysnatching incident took place between November and December in 1830 and was reported in the *Stamford Mercury*.

Today's view is part of the Crescent roundabout and encompasses the area from around where Cowgate ends, to looking back onto the locality outside the entrance to the collection point of John Lewis' department store – accessed via the Crescent roundabout.

GREAT NORTHERN HOTEL

THIS HOTEL IN Station Road is a railway hotel with all the elegance and charm of the Victorian period; it was designed in 1849 by the architect Henry Goddard of Lincoln. The hotel was built by Mr F. Costar at a cost of £2,500 and was opened on 1 April 1852.

To start with, it was the Great Northern Railway policy to put the management of its hotels out to tender and so staff were employed by the manager rather than the train company. However, after several disputes over the lease and the terms of the rental GNR took over management in the 1860s.

In 1857 the American novelist Nathaniel Hawthorne described his stay as 'wretched

and uncomfortable'. It took a change in management for things to improve and for standards to advance.

The records of chambermaid Laura Beken, who started work at the hotel in 1935, give us details about what the hotel was like in the late 1930s. Only the bathrooms had radiators and the front bedrooms were for single occupancy and were too small to have fireplaces, so guests had to be given hot-water bottles in the winter months. With the outbreak of the Second World War in September the hotel was closed to the public.

The hotel reopened in November 1949 after major repairs and in the 1950s it was a popular venue for wedding receptions. In the 1970s the building was extended to provide extra bedrooms and more banqueting and conference facilities. In 1982 the hotel was put up for sale by British Rail and after a number of owners it was bought by Peter Boizot (founder of Pizza Express). It is estimated that in 1993 he spent over £3 million on giving it a significant facelift. Today the hotel is owned by a consortium and boasts thirty-seven modern rooms.

CO-OPERATIVE BAKERY

HERE WE HAVE the full complement of builders posing for the photographer at the Peterborough & District Co-operative Society Ltd new bakery on the east side of Midland Road in 1928.

The old Co-op Bakery was located at No. 72–80 Cobden Street, but in 1927 it was judged to be too small for the expanding demand for bread and confectionery goods. The new bakery in Midland Road could bake nearly 5 million loaves (2lb in weight) annually, as nearly £100,000 was spent in installing the most modern machinery prior to the outbreak of the Second World War. In 1940 there were 140 employees with 100 working in the bakery itself. Over sixty

delivery vehicles were used and the manager at that time was Mr A. Davies.

The Co-op Dairy was on the same site and used to be one of the most up to date in the country, employing some 110 people. In 1939 over 1 million gallons of milk were taken in from 110 farms in Peterborough and its surrounding district.

Eventually the Co-op Bakery was sold to Rathbones and in November 2005 the business ceased trading, as it cost more to bake a loaf of bread than it did to buy one.

In April 2011 concerns were raised over the large amount of fly-tipped rubbish that was being dumped on the site and, in November 2010, fifty firefighters battled a blaze which tore through the dairy building; earlier that year the adjacent bakery was torched. In July 2012, Peterborough City Council were seeking to buy the derelict factory site from a firm of administrators as it had become an eyesore. The appearance and safety of the buildings became an issue for residents of Midland Road.

WEST TOWN SCHOOL

WEST TOWN SCHOOL in Williamson Avenue was opened as an infant school in 1909 and took 180 children. The headmistress in 1921, at the time of this photographic postcard, was Miss E. Drew of No. 84 Cromwell Road.

In May 2012, millions of pounds were pledged for the much-needed improvement works to West Town Primary School (which teaches infant and junior school children). About £2.3 million will be invested in the rebuilding or refurbishment which could provide more pupil places.

The Department of Education will provide the cash rather than the city council taxpayers, and some sort of private finance initiative will also be involved. This forms part of the government's Priority School Building Programme initiative.

Originally the school was built for the residents who had come to Peterborough because of the railways, engineering, agricultural and brick industries. The Great Northern Railway station (the only surviving station today) opened in August 1850 and employed a large number of blue-collar workers. The city started to grow and Victorian and Edwardian houses were built in Midland Road, Mayors Walk, Aldermans Drive, Percival Street, Clifton Avenue and Williamson Avenue.

The building of Williamson Avenue was proposed in 1877 and it was to have been called Allport Street after one of the directors of the Midland Railway (the Midland Railway line running adjacent to the Great Northern line to as far as Helpston). Subsequently the land was bought in 1906 and urbanised by a local and substantial furniture dealer by the name of Mr John Williamson. He was mayor of the city in 1915 (during the First World War) and was also chairman of the Municipal Electricity Board. John William Williamson died in 1936.

WOODSTON RECTORY

THIS IS THE vicarage adjacent to St Augustine's church on Oundle Road which stands on the site of a Saxon church. A fragment of the Saxon masonry still exists in the west wall of the church tower, in the shape of a tiny window. During the twelfth century, a belfry was added to the tower, and the church nave was given a south arcade in the thirteenth century. During the fourteenth century, a chancel was built (the present north wall of the chancel contains a doorway, near the nave, dating back to that time). The whole church fabric seems to have been in a sad state of repair in the early 1800s, and in 1840 most of the structure was rebuilt. By 1844 the church was fully restored having been rebuilt and refitted.

In the 1880s and 1890s the structure was developed further with the aisles being rebuilt and extended, and an organ chamber was added along with a north chapel and a vestry. A north porch was erected and the old south porch, which led to the burial churchyard, was blocked off. The existing structure is termed 'transition Norman style' with the walls being of coursed rubble, dressed with stone, and the roofing is of Colleyweston slate.

The rectory was refurbished and modified in the same style during the late nineteenth century. Over the centuries the parish of Woodston has had a number of noteworthy vicars – one of the earliest recorded was Walter de Glovernia, appointed in 1238 as the direct result of Royal Patronage.

Today the former rectory is privately owned and it has been occupied by Ian and Frances Benton and their family for nearly two decades. It is with their kind permission that we have the photograph of how the rectory looks today.

THE FIRST WORLD WAR –
PRECAUTION MEASURES

BRITAIN DECLARED WAR against Germany on 4 August 1914 following a sequence of events which had started that summer. Here, in August 1914, we see the National Telephone Co. in Queen Street, with its public telephone, using wire mesh as a protective and precautionary measure.

Not only were local businesses adapting to wartime, but local industries, too. Firms such as Frederick Sage & Co. Ltd of Walton produced aircraft (over 400 during the First World War – they were the first to produce aircraft with enclosed cockpits); Peter Brotherhood Ltd manufactured naval equipment; Werner, Pfleiderer & Perkins of Westwood Works produced, amongst other things, a number of engines and parts for tanks; Barford & Perkins of Queen

Street made road rollers and aeroplanes – the latter was considered to be top secret work; Baker Perkins produced munitions; J.P. Hall & Sons Ltd (established locally in 1899) manufactured boilers, pumps and pumping equipment for the navy.

Thus Peterborough was active in the war effort and its good rail connections made it ideal for the supply of such varied and extensive industrial equipment placed by government order.

It is interesting to note that anti-German feeling in Peterborough ran high at the start of the First World War and this led to the Riot Act being read in the city on Friday 7 August 1914 by the mayor, Richard Winfrey.

In October that year, for the sake of public peace, six German residents were asked to leave the city by the Chief Constable and a police escort took them by train to Leeman Road, York.

Today this part of Queen Street no longer exists as it was demolished to make way for Queensgate Shopping Centre, which was officially opened on 9 March 1982 by Queen Beatrix of the Netherlands, and contains nearly 100 stores with parking for about 2,500 cars.

CHURCH PARADE

HERE WE SEE the Northants Reserve Battery (J Company) of the Royal Field Artillery marching along Broadway towards the city centre on Sunday 25 October 1914. As with all elements of the regular army, these units were mobilised in August 1914 and were manned by a mixture of serving regulars, army and Special Reservists.

From October 1914 they began to be supplemented by wartime recruits and by the war's end, the majority of the regular units were not career soldiers. In general, the regular RFA units were under the command of the regular divisions until late 1915, when they were increasingly mixed into the New Army Divisions.

The soldiers are on their way to the cathedral. Enthusiastic passers-by, including women and children, cheer them on.

The procession is passing the former library on the western side of Broadway which is now Imperial Bento – a Chinese restaurant and Fever nightclub.

The former Public Library, a handsome red-brick building with stone facings, was given to the city by Andrew Carnegie and was opened by him on 29 May 1906 (the same day that he was made a Freeman of the City). It comprised a Reference Library, Lending Library, Children's Library and a special collection of Fenland and local literature. A general reading room contained a selection of newspapers, magazines and periodicals. There was also a large reference room which housed many maps of the district. Other branch libraries which opened later were Walton, which opened in 1937, Woodston, in 1951, and Dogsthorpe, in 1952.

This postcard is a poignant snapshot of a generation. Many of these volunteers and regulars would never make it back from fighting in the battlefields of France during the First World War – so their lives were cut short and their potential snuffed out.

TROOPS MARCHING IN PETERBOROUGH, 5TH NORFOLKS

HERE, THE 5TH Norfolks are marching south out of the city centre down Broad Bridge Street towards the river bridge. The entrance to Narrow Bridge Street can be seen in the centre background.

Before the town hall was built, the road's northern section from Albert Place to the Market Place (Cathedral Square) was called Narrow Bridge Street with the southern section being called Broad Bridge Street – sometimes referred to as Higher & Lower Bridge Street. In earlier times the whole street was called Hithegate.

The 5th Norfolks are now referred to as 'the vanished battalion'. They used to be known as 'The Sandringham Pals' because the majority of them were employed by the Royal Family at the Sandringham Estate. They trained in Colchester and Bury St Edmunds before being shipped out to Turkey.

The sad fate of how the majority perished in the First World War (21 August 1915 at Suvla) is described in Sir Ian Hamilton's despatch from the battlefield on 11 December 1915. He reported that the 5th Norfolks (the colonel, sixteen officers and 250 men) found themselves advancing and pushing on, driving the enemy away. Thereafter nothing more was ever seen or heard of any of them. They charged into the forest and were lost to sight and sound. None of them ever came back.

Thus the majority of the soldiers pictured in this photographic postcard came to a grisly end.

Only a few of the original buildings remain in what was Broad Bridge Street. Bourges Boulevard (the dual carriageway) can be seen in the immediate foreground of the present-day picture. It was so named in January 1965; Peterborough had been twinned with this French city in 1958. Bourges Boulevard was built in 1967–68 as an inner relief road.

FUNERAL OF AN ANZAC SOLDIER

SERGEANT C.T. HUNTER was born in Newcastle-upon-Tyne but emigrated to Australia in 1910 at the age of thirty. He settled in Broken Hill, a mining town in the outback of New South Wales, and spent four years working as a miner before enlisting with the Australian and New Zealand Army Corps (ANZAC) at the outbreak of the First World War.

Sergeant Thomas Hunter, known as 'The Lonely ANZAC', was one of the many thousands of brave men from Australia and New Zealand who took part in the disastrous Gallipoli landings in April 1915. He survived the bloody Gallipoli landings only to become one of the many casualties of

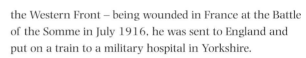

the Western Front – being wounded in France at the Battle of the Somme in July 1916, he was sent to England and put on a train to a military hospital in Yorkshire.

En route, his situation became critical and he was taken off at Peterborough, where he eventually died of spinal wounds at the Priestgate Hospital (now the city's museum) two days later on 31 July 1916. He was thirty-six years old.

The death of Sergeant Hunter of the 10th Australia Corp, New South Wales, so far from home, struck a chord with the people of Peterborough. He was buried with full military honours at the Broadway Cemetery and the chief mourners were led by the Mayor of Peterborough Councillor George Nicholls OBE JP, who took a special interest in this fallen soldier.

Today Sergeant Hunter's gravestone stands prominent in the cemetery and his grave is well preserved, as are many others. A group that champions the Broadway Cemetery site for both its local history and its wildlife is The Friends of Broadway Cemetery. They were founded in 2004 to campaign for the preservation and protection of the Victorian cemetery. The site has been a designated County Wildlife Site for over twenty-two years.

PETERBOROUGH WAR MEMORIAL HOSPITAL

THE FOUNDATION STONE to the War Memorial Hospital at the corner of Midland Road and
Thorpe Road was laid on 25 July 1925 – the previous building on the site was Thorpe Lawn
(a private house which then became the first meeting place of the British Legion). The site
was generously given to the people of Peterborough by Alderman Bunting of Spalding (former
Peterborough resident and Freeman of the City).

The Memorial Hospital cost £70,000–£80,000 to build and was established as a voluntary
hospital from public contributions made after the First World War and was officially opened
on 14 June 1928 by Field Marshal Sir William Robertson. The children's hospital to the south

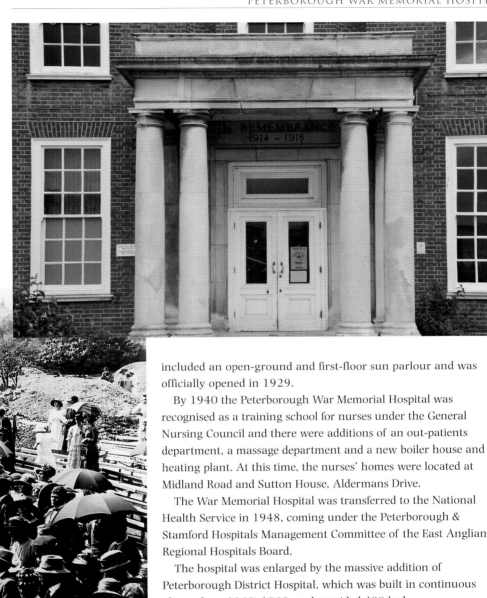

included an open-ground and first-floor sun parlour and was officially opened in 1929.

By 1940 the Peterborough War Memorial Hospital was recognised as a training school for nurses under the General Nursing Council and there were additions of an out-patients department, a massage department and a new boiler house and heating plant. At this time, the nurses' homes were located at Midland Road and Sutton House, Aldermans Drive.

The War Memorial Hospital was transferred to the National Health Service in 1948, coming under the Peterborough & Stamford Hospitals Management Committee of the East Anglian Regional Hospitals Board.

The hospital was enlarged by the massive addition of Peterborough District Hospital, which was built in continuous phases from 1960–1968, and provided 400 beds.

Presently the site is empty because of the City Hospital in Bretton Gate which opened in the winter of 2010. However, Peterborough City Council planning officers have developed initial proposals in partnership with property specialists, King Sturge, to redevelop the site. The idea is to have a mix of family houses, apartments and small shops. The outline scheme suggests retaining historic buildings such as the core part of the Memorial Hospital and improving the pedestrian and cycle routes.

EVICTION

IN NOVEMBER 1918, Prime Minister Lloyd George promised to make Britain a fit country for heroes to live in. It fell to Christopher Addison (born in the neighbouring county of Lincolnshire) to devise and carry out the policy by which homes would be provided for the men returning from the First World War. The Housing and Town Planning Act of 1919 gave local authorities the power to build unlimited numbers of houses at low and controlled rents with their losses being met by government subsidy.

Christopher Addison's 'Homes for Heroes' programme was meant to provide quality houses for the working classes and for returning soldiers and their families. Instead, the 1920s showed that governments needed to be wary of making promises they could not keep as private and local authority rents increased, making it impossible for tenants to afford their homes.

Little maintenance and renovation work was performed during and after the First World War – yet rents continued to increase.

Guaranteeing to build houses on an unprecedented scale was good for short-term political popularity, but the target of half a million houses to be built in three years proved highly unrealistic.

Unfortunately only half were completed and in 1923, with the Conservatives in power, it was replaced by Neville Chamberlain's Housing Act, which reduced the subsidies and placed more emphasis on the private sector. In 1924 the Labour Government's Wheatey Act replaced that of the Conservative Housing Act. These Acts did nevertheless manage to create 580,000 new homes by 1935.

This was, of course, no consolation to individuals who found themselves literally out on the streets with no roof over their heads and no means of affording one in a pre-social security benefits era.

This family sits outside No. 40 Cromwell Road with various household items such as a washing tub and mangle, table and chairs, bedding, a settee and pots and pans and a few bags of clothing. Their faces say it all – one wonders today what fate awaited them.

Today this particular block of terraced houses has been demolished and replaced with 1920s and '30s homes. It's possible that the original bricks from the Victorian terraced house were used to build the front garden wall outside the existing No. 40 Cromwell Road.

TOPOGRAPHICAL SCENE

HERE IS A wonderful Edwardian street scene with cyclists, a horse-drawn carriage and a woman taking a baby for a walk in a perambulator.

Eastfield at this time was described as being near Peterborough but was mainly rural. Its principal residents were Messrs Thomas Fevre, Josiah Searson, John Smith, Joshua Taylor, and Dr J. Walker. Also located in Eastfield were the nurseries belonging to Messrs A. & Charles Peach and W. & J. Brown. The tram from the city centre terminus in Long Causeway took you along the whole of Eastfield Road to the Newark terminus. You can see the tram lines in the road and the overhead tram wires on the right.

Today's view of Eastfield Road is very different. The entrance to Peterborough Regional College (formerly Peterborough Technical College) is on the left – just past the traffic lights. In 1946

temporary classrooms and laboratories were provided at Garton End Road and Mr C. Fenton was appointed as the first principal. In 1952 proposals for a larger technical college went out to tender. Mr D. Jenkin was awarded the contract and later that year the first phase of the Technical College was completed on land adjacent to the East of England showground; Mr John McIntyre was appointed principal.

On 1 October 1953 the building was officially opened by the Right Honourable Lord Percy of Newcastle. During this time, full use was being made not only of these new premises but also of the temporary buildings in Garton End Road and three other schools. It was evident that an extension was needed.

In 1955 Messrs Portess & Richardson were appointed as architects for the second phase. Financial donations were received by Baker Perkins Ltd for the building of a General Science laboratory, by the Peter Brotherhood Ltd for a Physics laboratory, by AEI – Hotpoint Ltd – for a General Science laboratory and by Frank Perkins Ltd for a motor vehicle workshop to be built.

In 1958 the extension was occupied and the Technical College stopped using the Garton End Road premises and the old school in New Road. From then on, all classes were at Eastfield Road. In 1959 the engineering block was extended and plans for a third instalment to include an Assembly Hall began.

Nowadays the college offers higher education courses and has a University Centre affiliated to Anglia Ruskin University, Cambridge.

AGRICULTURAL SOCIETY'S SHOWGROUND

HERE IS THE entrance to the showground at Eastfield. The Society offices were in Cross Street and every year the society would hold a three-day show in July.

Eastfield in 1912 was outside the Borough boundary and was located north-east of the city centre. Prior to 1911 the showground was located at Millfield on a site behind the windmill, and the grounds stretched as far as Taverners Road. This land was owned by the Ecclesiastical Commissioners. However, in 1909 the society was told that this land would be required for building purposes so they looked around for another site and ended up purchasing 24 acres at a cost of £2,495.

Combined with the three-day agricultural show (held from the third Tuesday in July) was the three-day National Foxhound & Beagle show. The society also had seasonal shows, including a Stallion show in the spring and a Mare & Foal show in the autumn.

The president of the Peterborough Agricultural Society in 1912 was Lord Lilford (John Powys 1863–1945). Honorary members included Mr William Horrell, Mr Thomas Stokes and Mr G. Morris. The society was formed at a meeting held at the Angel Inn, Narrow Bridge Street, on 10 January 1797. Its first president was Earl Fitzwilliam.

A permanent grandstand was built at the Eastfield site in 1936, with seating for 2,000 people, at a cost of £7,000. By 1954 the Eastfield showground occupied 46 acres.

His Majesty King Edward VII, while he was Prince of Wales, visited the show (then located in the Park Road/Broadway area) in 1878 and also in the following year. In July 1898 the Prince of Wales was president of the Peterborough Foxhound & Beagle show. Many members of the Royal Family have been regular visitors to the show over the years – including the late Queen Mother, as well as Her Majesty Queen Elizabeth II, the Duke of Edinburgh, and Charles, the Prince of Wales. Indeed, Her Majesty the Queen (whilst she was Princess Elizabeth) was president of the society when it was sited at Eastfield. Edward, Prince of Wales (later His Majesty King Edward VIII who abdicated in 1936) visited the Eastfield showground in 1923.

In 1965 the show moved to its present site at Alwalton.

The Eastfield Road entrance is now in the vicinity of Delamere Close and its surrounds.

FLETTON

THIS PICTURE POSTCARD shows No. 36 Fletton Avenue in the right foreground and Nos 33 and 35 Fletton Avenue in the left foreground. Following the road round to the centre left would take you to Joseph Farrow & Co. Ltd, who were allied to agriculture concerns and made canned foods (green peas, later marrowfat peas) at their Carlton Works in Fletton.

Joseph Farrow's Canning Factory gave work to a large number of females, mostly processing peas, for which they were most noted, but also other fruits and vegetables when in season. As a subsidiary of Reckitt & Colman they also produced mushroom ketchup and mustard. The Joseph Farrow works site located at the end of where Fellowes Road is today was subsequently taken over by Frank Perkins diesel manufacturers in the 1970s.

Fletton can be traced back to at least Norman times when the whole township or manor of Fletton belonged to the Abbey of Peterborough.

In 1615, the lords of Fletton were the Feoffees of Oliver Harvey, but in 1628 the title passed to Francis and Oliver

Saye. In 1671 Sir Humphrey Winch was lord, and the steward of Fletton was James Gates, an ancestor of the first mayor of Peterborough – Henry Pearson Gates.

Fletton Avenue links the London Road to Fletton High Street and the road which was built in 1891/92 followed a line of seven large Elm trees, known locally as the 'Seven Sisters'.

Principal residents in the Edwardian era included Mr John William Claypole of No. 5 Fletton Avenue, who owned Claypole's Music shop at No. 55 Narrow Bridge Street; Mr Claude Isch-Wall of No. 48 Fletton Avenue, who was the manager at Celta Mills – the flax factory in Woodston; Mr Thomas Hunting of No. 52 Fletton Avenue, who was the manager at Coote & Warren Ltd – the coal wagon merchants; Mr George Rippon of No. 15 Fletton Avenue, who owned Rippons the builders merchants in Queens Street; and the Revd Gustavus Mees of No. 9 Fletton Avenue who was the Wesleyan Chapel Minister.

Today many of these houses remain, but with double-glazed windows and front garden walls bereft of iron railings. The road has fewer elm trees along it and the abundance of parked cars and traffic makes it a much busier scene than that of over a century ago.

FLETTON

THIS ROAD LINKS London Road to the Fletton by-pass road at Stanground. In this 1930s postcard of Fletton High Street the photographer has taken the shot just past Kings Road, which is out of view in the left foreground. The turn, centre left, takes you to Fleet Way, a cul-de-sac off Fletton High Street. The Fleet is the stream that runs into Stanground Lode. It is from the name of this stream that the township of Fletton derives its name.

The turn past the second telegraph pole on the right takes you onto Fletton Avenue. The house in the immediate left foreground belonged to Henry Longfoot, and next door at No. 67 lived Percy Ireland. No. 42 High Street is on the right and was the newsagents and general store run by Horace Ibbott. Next door to that is the general dealer Mr Strickson. Today No. 67 Fletton High Street has been demolished and a relatively modern building has been erected.

Left of centre in the 1930s postcard is the White Hart Inn, advertising Warwick's Newark Ales and Stout on draught. It was located at No. 77 High Street and was run at this time by Mr Arthur Brown.

The building next but one before the turning into Fleet Way, centre left, is the general store run by Reginald Stocker at No. 75 High Street. Next to his shop is the Court House, once occupied by Police Sergeant Bradford. Past the White Hart Inn can be found the Old Fletton Urban District Council offices located at No. 79.

Today on Fleet Way can be found the Fleet Centre, which is run by the Italian Community Association. The Italian community in Peterborough established themselves here in the 1950s – settling in areas like Stanground and Fletton, as they mainly worked in the brickyards owned by London Brick Co.

The present-day view still shows a parade of shops along the right-hand side but you can still see the front-garden entrance to No. 65 Fletton High Street. However, the terraced houses with their dormer windows on the immediate left in the 1932 photograph have since been demolished to make way for new homes that are just out of shot in the immediate left foreground of the present-day photograph.

DOGSTHORPE

THERE HAS BEEN a brickmaking tradition in the Peterborough area from as far back as the eighteenth century. These tended to be small yards, operating on a seasonal basis and using shallow clays. It wasn't until the 1880s that testing with the lower-lying Oxford Clay allowed bricks to be produced on an industrial scale. These new bricks fostered competition between several companies all aiming to exploit the new process, which in turn encouraged many larger companies to buy out the smaller brickmaking yards.

Dogsthorpe brickworks, to the north of Welland Road, were owned by Edward Vergette in the 1860s; then Thomas Parker from 1872 to 1890, and then George Cursley from 1890 to 1897. In 1897 the site was sold to John William Rowe, who started the Dogsthorpe Brick & Tile Co. Ltd. However, two years later it would appear that the entire site was put up for auction but did not sell.

Thus, it is the more unusual partnership between John William Rowe and Matilda Hill (the wife of John Cathles Hill) that this vintage photographic postcard celebrates.

Apparently, it was Mrs Hill who provided Rowe with a significant portion of the money he needed to purchase a plot of land for the brickworks at Dogsthorpe level crossing in 1899 (Dogsthorpe Site II). From 1899 they traded as the Star Pressed Brick Co. The company completed several important local orders, including the supply of bricks for the Baker Perkins factories (1904–7), Peter Brotherhoods factory (1906–7), and the factory of Frederick Sage & Co. Ltd (1911).

In 1904, Rowe and Mrs Hill bought a 19-acre site at Kings Dyke, Whittlesey, where they established another works – the Star Pressed Brick Co. (Whittlesey) Ltd.

John Rowe's interest and involvement in the brick and lime industries came from his business as a local builders' merchant. He put great store in the quality of his materials (ornamental bricks, tiles and drainage pipes) and subsequently, in 1897, he bought a small brickyard (Dogsthorpe Site I). Two years later he bought land three quarters of a mile further down the road (Dogsthorpe Site II) with Mrs Hill. He also had an interest in the lime industry and owned kilns at Walton, Peterborough.

Today the site is close to the Householders Recycling Centre in Welland Road.

MILLFIELD

THIS WINDMILL WAS known locally as Adam's Mill due to a former owner. In 1884 John Adams, miller and baker, owned the mill, as well as the one in New Fletton. Before this the mill was better known as the Peterborough Tower Mill and in the 1770s was run by William Dodson; by 1781 the owner was Thomas Pepper.

In 1909 the mill was being worked by James Garner and the shop on the left at No. 218 Lincoln Road was that of Edward James Quemby, a corn merchant's manager and shop owner. The shop sold Melox, a concentrated meal for dogs, and other dog food brands like Spratts and Mixed Marvels. The Peterborough & District Directory yearbook still has Quemby listed at the same premises in 1922. The slogan on the advertising sign says: 'Every happy family owns a happy dog if fed on Melox and Mixed Marvels "The Food of the Dogs".'

This area of Lincoln Road was the site of the Peterborough Agricultural Society's showground until the lease ran out in 1909. The Ecclesiastical

Commissioners who owned the land decided to sell it to enable the area to be developed as a residential estate. Millfield was the site of the town gallows in the days of the monastery; prisoners condemned to capital punishment by the Abbott's Justices were executed here.

The old Windmill Inn located at No. 281 Lincoln Road was left derelict and nearly destroyed by fire in September 2010. It then became the subject of various planning applications to convert the premise into either a shop or residential property. The windmill was demolished in 1937. Originally it had six sails, an ogee cap, a six-bladed fantail and a stage. It was converted to electricity in 1915, the same year that it lost its unique set of six sails. The pub used to have a clubroom for a sing-song of a weekend.

Today's view is that of a petrol station and store.

NEW ENGLAND

THE CHURCH OF St Paul's was known locally as the Railwayman's church. In the latter half of the nineteenth century, New England was slowly being converted from a rural area into one of industry, thanks to the arrival of the railways and the engine sheds.

Following the building of the Mission Hall a more ambitious project started to take shape (the GNR made a grant of £50 a year and also provided a vicarage for the rector). St Paul's church was the outcome. The Ecclesiastical Commissioners gave 1½ acres of land and the railway directors also contributed money towards the building of a church. The church of St Paul was duly consecrated on Friday 28 May 1869 by Bishop William Canon Magee – later Archbishop of York.

The first vicar was Canon C.R. Ball, who donated the Fountain at New England in November 1884. He then went on to become Vicar of All Saints in 1886. From 1886 until 1933, the vicar was Canon A.F. Maskew, who died in 1938; his remains are interred at Paston church.

Succeeding vicars were Revd F.J. Boss (1933–1943), Revd J.A. Fisher (1943–1953), and then Revd D.M. Forrester, who in 1958 was the overseer of some expensive renovations work at a cost of £6,000 – an interesting sum when you consider that the initial cost of the building was £4,000.

Gifts and improvements over the years produced a porch in 1887, a vestry in 1902, a hall in 1905, and an oak pulpit in 1937. A new high altar was added in 1950 in memory of Canon Maskew.

In 2007–8, a new 8ft-high steel cross was erected on the roof of St Paul's and the bells were overhauled. On Saturday 12 December 2009, the dedication of the cross and bell service was undertaken by Canon Gordon Steele, the Rural Dean and Vicar of Peterborough parish church, St John the Baptist.

The vicarage looks to have been a splendid Victorian property in this postcard from around 1907. It was located between the recreation ground and the church. One can only imagine that the double horse-drawn carriage is awaiting its occupant – Canon Maskew.

Sadly the vicarage was demolished to make way for a new one at No. 414 Lincoln Road.

NEW ENGLAND

THIS CHURCH ON Lincoln Road was built at a cost of £600 by Messrs Dawson of Spalding and could accommodate 300 people. The foundation stone was laid on 12 September 1865 and the chapel was officially opened on 5 April 1866. The Sunday school opened in March 1903.

There were many Wesleyan chapels in Peterborough and its surrounding villages, but the largest was in Wentworth Street, which had a seating capacity of 900. It was acquired in 1834 and rebuilt in 1874.

Wesleyan Methodism began in 1739 and John Wesley was an early leader of this Protestant Christian movement. He was born in Epworth, North Lincolnshire – some 13 miles from Scunthorpe.

It is interesting to note that few substantial buildings existed in New England in 1850, except for the Railway Loco sheds, which were then under construction and were only completed in 1853. The land for the railway cottages was purchased by the

GNR from the Bishop of Peterborough in 1852. These cottages were built in five separate phases to accommodate the railway workers and their families.

The first cottages built in 1854 were known as Gas House Row – erected in the opposite direction to the ones that followed. They were built east to west and were in line with the cinder path of the steam trains. Eventually they were demolished between 1892 and 1893 to make way for extensions to the Railway Yards.

The second group of cottages were built in 1856 by Messrs Holmes & Rumnies. The third group and school were built by Messrs Dale of Louth, and the fourth group and the Mission Hall were built by Messrs Dawson of Spalding in 1863. The same company completed the fifth group of cottages and this Wesleyan Methodist chapel in 1866. Thus a total of 250 cottages formed a miniature town with no shops. Millfield was the nearest shopping centre with a chemist, newsagent, grocery store and the mill.

Presently the New Testament Church of God occupies the site but in the past it has been used by other faiths.

WALTON

THIS ROAD USED to take you from Lincoln Road to the village of Marholm, where there was a level crossing. This view is looking 100 yards down towards Lincoln Road with your back towards the crossing. Today Marholm Road is a cul-de-sac that can only be reached from The Mead, off Lincoln Road.

Nearby was the factory and offices of Frederick Sage & Co. Ltd who had an entrance to their factory off Sages Lane. They started as a London-based quality shop-fitting business, but grew and had international offices and factories in South Africa, Belgium, France and Germany.

To cope with the increased volume of trade, a new factory was built at Walton in 1910 and it covered an area of 100,000 sq. ft. This site was chosen because of its proximity to the railway, which provided significant transport links to the main shipping ports in the country.

In 1915, during the First World War, the company placed its resources at the disposal of the British Government and it entered into a contract with the Admiralty for a number of seaplanes designed by the Short Co. The first of these planes was in the air within three months.

From then until the end of hostilities the company applied itself to the war effort – manufacturing Short Seaplanes, Avro Training Machines, and SE5 airframes for the fledgling Royal Navy Air Service (RNAS). The Peterborough factory turned out an average of 100 planes a year, and Sage of Walton were the first to produce aircraft with an enclosed cockpit. (See inset of the Sage Type 2 plane.)

Their greatest success came when their own aircraft design team built seaplanes which were adopted as the basic RNAS training craft for 1919. The Walton factory briefly returned to aircraft production during the Second World War, as Sage's company was acquired by the Aeronautical Corporation of Great Britain in 1936.

In 1961, the Walton factory was still in existence and employed architectural metal craftsmen and contractors who produced shop and store fittings for shopfronts and showcases. More recently, the factory was used by Frank Perkins, and later Triplex Machining Ltd, to produce autoparts for General Motors. Today nothing remains of the 6-acre factory site except the water tower (Sage's Tower), which acts as a landmark.

The view of Marholm Road today shows that many of the front garden fences have gone, but part of the old telegraph pole remains.

LONGTHORPE

IN 1850 THORPE Hall was derelict. The new purchaser – the Revd William Strong (of Longthorpe Tower) – had bought Thorpe Hall estate from Earl Fitzwilliam. He set to updating the hall, but Strong's alterations and renewal in the Italian style didn't detract from its original Cromwellian mansion design by John Webb (nephew of architect Inigo Jones).

The building dates back to Oliver St John (1598–1673), a Lord Chief Justice who supported Parliament in the Civil War, and who bought the freehold of some 26 hectares in Longthorpe in 1653. Oliver St John had Thorpe Hall built from 1650 onwards out of the ruins of Peterborough Cathedral's Bishop's Palace and cloister, mixed with stone from Barnack quarries. Thorpe Hall was finally completed in 1656 by the builder Peter Mills.

The mid-seventeenth-century architect John Webb (1611–1672) went to great pains to vary both the design and the material of Thorpe Hall. Together with local stone he used various types of marble.

The Grade I listed house sits in 5–6 acres of garden and outbuildings and in the mid-nineteenth century the Revd William Strong extended the walled garden to the west, creating a large kitchen garden and two new lodges. There were two entrance courts – one by road to the north and the other by water access to the south from the river Nene. Pairs of lead falcons used to adorn both sets of gates.

On the death of Revd William Strong, the seat of Thorpe Hall was passed to his elder son Lieutenant-Colonel Charles Isham Strong (1838–1914). Upon Charles' death, his eldest son, Brigadier General Strong, took over the running of Thorpe Hall from 1914 until 1927, when it was acquired by the Meaker family.

The Grade II listed gardens were fully restored in 1989 and they retain the old urns and gates, but the planting is post-1990.

From 1943 to 1970 Thorpe Hall was used as a Maternity Hospital. It was acquired by the Sue Ryder Foundation in 1986, and opened in May 1991 as a hospice, and remains so today.

In November 2011, the Sue Ryder Foundation was granted planning permission to build a new state-of-the-art single-storey hospice within the existing grounds. The view today is the main entrance to Thorpe Hall and it appears plain and without any architectural grandeur.

LONGTHORPE

A WONDERFUL PERIOD view of Thorpe Road with the garage at No. 347 in the immediate right foreground. In 1936 this was owned by Mrs Harriet Colbert. The lane to the left is Grove Lane, and the Fox & Hounds public house's car park is just out of shot of the left foreground.

This is a very rural view of this part of Thorpe Road. One can see Longthorpe Tower, attached to the Manor House, in the distance and there are hardly any houses to be seen.

Today the garage is a TWG Motor Sports Garage. Since 1982 they have been involved in providing quality and dependable care of Porsches, BMWs, and Mercedes cars. They specialise in mechanical repair and maintenance, as well as providing quality control schemes.

Longthorpe Tower, the three-storey tower in the distance, was added in 1310 to the Longthorpe fortified manor house of 1263, which was a farmhouse for about 500 years from the mid-1400s. The last agricultural occupier of Longthorpe Tower and manor house was Hugh

Horrell, and it was he who found the famous wall paintings when decorating in 1946. The paintings are said to be the most comprehensive of any domestic medieval building in England (and possibly Europe) and they display a range of biblical, monastic and secular subjects.

The tower section of the manor house was possibly erected by Robert de Thorpe, steward of Peterborough Abbey from 1330, and tenant of the building.

The paintings are generally dated to around 1330, with the decoration covering all the walls, the window splays and the vault. In the vault are the four *Evangelist Symbols* and *David with his Musicians*.

Longthorpe Tower was given to the nation by Captain Fitzwilliam under the Ancient Monuments Act of 1913. The Tower is now the responsibility of English Heritage. The Tower House itself was sold in 1981 along with a single-building plot, fit for a bungalow. The remaining agricultural buildings, previously part of Tower Farm and Tower House, were sold separately for conversion to private dwellings.

THE SANATORIUM

THE CITY'S ISOLATION hospital, also known as the Sanatorium, was built on the site of Low Farm – the ancient grange of the Peterborough Abbey's Chamberlain. It was opened in 1901 for infectious diseases and had thirty-two beds, but by 1940 it could only accommodate twenty-five patients. At that time Miss Skinner was the matron, along and with a staff of six nurses and five domestics. In 1952 the isolation hospital had twenty-seven beds and was very successful in the treatment of all types of infections, including poliomyelitis.

It is easy to forget just how many infectious diseases were rampant before the advent of antibiotics. Each town or city would have facilities, usually away from other hospitals or buildings, for the isolation and treatment of diseases such as diphtheria, polio, cholera, typhoid, and smallpox. Tuberculosis was common and with few treatments other than rest, good nutrition and fresh air, isolation hospitals or sanatoriums, like the one in Fengate, were home to many long-term sufferers. Often, the natural resources of the area in which a sanatorium was located, such as clean air or mineral springs, were used as part of the treatment or cure.

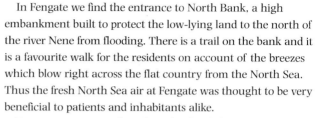

In Fengate we find the entrance to North Bank, a high embankment built to protect the low-lying land to the north of the river Nene from flooding. There is a trail on the bank and it is a favourite walk for the residents on account of the breezes which blow right across the flat country from the North Sea. Thus the fresh North Sea air at Fengate was thought to be very beneficial to patients and inhabitants alike.

During winter months, when the flooded fields around the North Bank were frozen over, it was reported that skaters from across the area would find sheets of ice second to none.

The hospital eventually shut down in 1981, but had long since been closed to patients with infectious diseases. Instead, it was a hospital (renamed St Peter's Hospital) for those with behavioural and learning difficulties.

Today, the roundabout takes you from Fengate onto Potters Way where there's a new development called Connect 21, which provides three-, four- and five-storey buildings in a series of crescents, squares and terraces built by Kier Homes. The developer boasts that the area offers houses and flats for every kind of living idea, style and price.

WOODSTON

THIS POSTCARD SHOWS Palmerston Road looking towards New Road. The opening on the right leads to the Jetty – a pathway that came out on Oundle Road between the Boy's Head public house (now the Boro Pub) and St Augustine's church. The fencing, centre right, shows the front gardens of the linked houses named Demontfort Terrace, and in the immediate right foreground is the off-licence at No. 84 Palmerston Road with its stout advertisement showing. In 1908 the licensee was Mr J. Grice.

A little over a century ago Woodston had an active community life that was centred around the 'Palmerston Road Room' – renamed the Parish Room in 1889. It also acted as a polling station for the County & Soke of Peterborough.

During the golden age of British Railways – from the late nineteenth century until the early twentieth century – many Woodston people were employed by the railway companies. In May 1889,

Mr Smith (foreman shunter) suffered the loss of a leg and Mr Adams, another Woodston resident and Sunday-school teacher, was killed while on duty in Cambridge.

In August 1890 it was reported that the postmaster general had agreed that the name of the post office be changed from New Fletton to Woodstone (the old spelling of the village).

A happy event was the 'Annual Treat' of the Sunday schools, which involved the youngsters being entertained on the lawn of St Augustine's vicarage and in the paddock behind. Parents went off to Alwalton Lynch for the day and local tradesmen and other residents provided the transport which included coal carts – scrubbed clean – provided by Mr Hunting. The most sought after was the Co-op bread van because it was clean and drawn by a horse that ran.

Activities at the vicarage included the provision of afternoon tea, where huge amounts of bread, butter and cakes were consumed and washed down by gallons of tea.

The winter months in Woodston saw the annual floods at Wharf Road (Water End) occur. These extended as far as the Ferry Boat Inn. When frozen over, the area provided an excellent skating and sliding rink.

Today the off-licence premises are a residential property and there's a relatively new block of flats and houses on the same side where the picket fence was – but the Victorian terraces remain in the left foreground.

ORTON LONGUEVILLE

A SPLENDID LATE 1960s view of leisure boats moored along the river embankment at Orton Longueville; along with yachts out on the river with the PYC's clubhouse, seen centre right. The club was set up to encourage and promote sailing and yachting. At the time of this postcard there were two racing periods: winter time in home waters and summer time above Orton Staunch. The 'Amies' cup competition was held every six months and the Cock Burgee and Cup was competed annually.

Boat owners paid an annual subscription of 10s and non-boat owners 18s 6d in 1969. Annual meetings were held in the clubhouse from 15–30 September.

Today the view is just as animated and this pastime appears to remain as popular as ever.

Orton Longueville was a village separated from the city by open farmland until the 1960s. It is home to Orton Longueville School – now Nene Park Academy. The village contains many

pre-twentieth century buildings including Orton Hall – once the seat of the Marquess of Huntly; it is now a Best Western Hotel. In the Second World War it was used as a Prisoner of War camp. There are several thatched cottages, a cricket field, a mixed school, Holy Trinity church, and the Gordon Arms public house.

Orton Longueville Manor belonged to the Lovetofts and then passed through various hands until the Gordons (Marquis of Huntly) took it over as Orton Hall estate.

Trinity church was built in the Early English style. It boasts a tower and has an old fresco of St Christopher along with monuments to the Cope and Gordon families. One of the most notable residents was Francis 'Frank' Buckle (1767–1832). He was a champion jockey whose record was not beaten until the arrival of Lester Piggott over 120 years later. Frank lived on his farm at Botolph in Orton Longueville and is buried at Holy Trinity church. He continued to ride until his death at the age of sixty-five in 1832.

The present Botolph Arms pub is thought to sit on the farm Frank owned which, during his time, had substantial fields attached to it. Today, Frank's sarcophagus can be located within the burial grounds of Trinity church, but it looks rather neglected and overgrown with ivy.

ORTON WATERVILLE

ORTON WATERVILLE AT this time was a village three miles south-west of the city. It was half a mile to the railway station at Overton on the London and North Western railway line. The population was mainly engaged in agriculture, but prior to the turn of the nineteenth century many were employed in the stone quarries and gravel pits which became exhausted at the end of the 1890s.

The church is dedicated to St Mary the Virgin and dates from before the early twelfth century. The manor at Orton Waterville was passed from Archbishop Booth (Archbishop of York) to Pembroke College in 1408 and the college master and college fellows became the lords of the manor. There used to be a mixed National School but this is now a private residence.

Cherry Orton Road was so named because of the cherry orchards and the cottage with dormer windows which remains thatched to this day – having Grade II listed building status. The parish church was founded by the Waterville family as a private residence and it was rebuilt at the end of the thirteenth century.

In 1861 Roman mosaics and other remains were dug up – indicating that a Roman villa had once occupied the area.

Several explanations have been put forward as to the origins of the name Cherry Orton (the name before it became Orton Waterville) and a will from 1504 says that Cherry Week was an established and recognised annual event.

At No. 29 Cherry Orton Road sits the Windmill public house which is virtually opposite the thatched cottage on the 1921 postcard. The pub was once the residence of Private Stanley Hodson of the 6th Battalion, Northamptonshire Regiment who was killed in action at Trones Wood during the Battle of the Somme on 14 July 1916, aged twenty. His name can be found on the Thiepval Memorial in Picardie, France. In 1921 the landlady was Mrs Hodson (presumably the widow of Stanley).

Records from 1936 show that there were 1,399 acres of land and that Overton station was then on the London, Midland & Scottish Railway.

Today the Windmill pub is run by TLC Inns, who are an independent family-run company.

ALWALTON

THIS POSTCARD SHOWS the Wheat Sheaf Inn with St Andrew's church in the background. In 1909 Alwalton was a small agricultural village about four miles from Peterborough. Wansford was the nearest railway station and the population was about 200.

In 1279 the abbot of Peterborough held the manor of Alwalton and the village, which at that time had three water mills and a common fish pond with a weir on the bank of the river Nene that started at Wildlake and extended to the mill at Water Newton.

There was an earlier church on the site of the St Andrews which dates back to 1170. During the early thirteenth century the church was extended, a tower was built and the nave lengthened. It's likely that the carving around the west door was done at the same time.

The Wheat Sheaf inn has also had various internal and external reordering over time, as well as some famous visitors. It is said that Clark Gable, the famous Hollywood actor, was a frequent

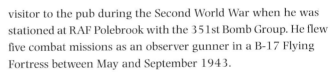

visitor to the pub during the Second World War when he was stationed at RAF Polebrook with the 351st Bomb Group. He flew five combat missions as an observer gunner in a B-17 Flying Fortress between May and September 1943.

Alwalton village was the birthplace of the famous Frederick Henry Royce (born 27 March 1863) who was the youngest of five children of James and Mary Royce. Henry Royce lived in Alwalton until the family moved to London when he was aged four. He returned Peterborough at the age of fourteen to work as an apprentice at the Great Northern Railway Works – becoming an electrical engineer. Henry went on to build the first Royce 10hp car in 1903–4 before becoming the co-founder of Rolls Royce. A plaque to his memory can be found in the church.

Another prominent resident was Francis Arthur Perkins, the founder of Perkins Engines (world famous for diesel engines). Frank Perkins lived at Alwalton Hall until his death on 15 October 1967 – he and his wife are interred in St Andrew's churchyard.

Alwalton is a conservation area and the 1909 view has changed little today except that the trees obscure the church, the picket fence has gone and dormer windows have been added to the pub, which is now called the Cuckoo.

WERRINGTON

THIS 1960s POSTCARD shows the village sign standing proud on the village green. In the early Victorian period Werrington is described as a village in the parish of Paston. Its nearest railway station was located at Walton. In the 1870s its population was 697 with 161 houses. In 1876 Werrington separated from Paston.

In the 1950s and '60s Werrington was engulfed by the city. There are two distinct areas of Werrington – the village in Werrington South and New Werrington, referred to as Werrington North. South Werrington is the historical part and focuses on the village green. North Werrington focuses on Werrington Centre – a small shopping complex with a supermarket and other retail outlets.

The church of St John the Baptist was built in the Early English style but it has narrow Norman arches and the inner door dates back to Norman times. The church grounds lack any ancient gravestones – there is nothing earlier than the mid-nineteenth century. This is because prior to 1851 the deceased were laid to rest in nearby Paston.

At one point the church fell into disrepair and for a while part of the nave was exposed to the elements, meaning urgent works had to be undertaken. Repairs took place in 1680 under the oversight of the churchwardens – Robert West and John Holden. The porch dates back to 1668.

Werrington has a mill located in the area of Sharma Leas and the Paddocks (off Lincoln Road) which was built in 1864 – although the base dates back to an earlier 'smock mill' that was on the site from the 1600s until it burnt down in the 1830s.

Two of the mill's sails were lost in the 1912 storm and the remaining two were removed in 1920. The mill continued to provide steam power up until 1953 when the last of the millers (Earnest Goff) retired. After this date the mill continued to serve a purpose as storage for a local business. In more recent times it has been stripped of its outer tar layer and has been lovingly restored as living accommodation.

WERRINGTON

IN THE IMMEDIATE right foreground is the Three Horse Shoes pub, Church Street. Its first recorded landlord was Thomas Lynn in 1841 and he remained landlord until his death in 1874. As well as being the pub landlord he was also the blacksmith. In 1877 the pub was rebuilt and just past the pub on the right-hand side can be seen the old fire-engine house that served Walton and Werrington. Amberley Slope, which now departs to the right, follows the course of an old narrow lane that led to Werrington's famous cherry orchards.

Twenty years before this 1918 postcard, Werrington had a recorded population of 740 with 196 houses. It also had a mixed National School and a post office run by Mrs Barnes. At this time there was a Primitive Methodist Chapel as well as a Wesleyan Methodist chapel in addition to the Church of England, St John the Baptist church, whose vicar in 1898 was the Revd Charles Holdich. The nearest railway station was at Walton (Midland Railway).

Some principal occupants at the turn of the last century were farmers: Joseph Serjeant; Martin Odam (of the Manor House); Robert Dyson; John Goodman; and Robert Hadman. The parish clerk was George Pitts and the schoolmaster was Mr J. Wright, who lived at Sydney Villa.

The chairman of Werrington Parish Council at this time was Mr Joseph Serjeant (farm owner). Apart from the parish clerk mentioned above – other members included: Robert Hadman (dairyman and farmer); Thomas Rose (farm bailiff); Thomas Pratt (tailor); John Searle (shopkeeper); George Tyler (butcher), and owner of Werrington Mill Ernest Goff (miller and baker).

Today the dirt-track road on the right of the 1918 view is Amberley Slope and to the immediate left, in the foreground, is the turning to Pipistrelle Court – so named because of the bats that frequented the locality.

Some recent residents of Werrington (of less than ten years) tend to call the Three Horse Shoes pub 'The Slaughtered Lamb' apparently because of the very 'locals only' vibe it used to have. However, these days it has come under new management and is said to be more welcoming. Everyone is invited to join in with the fun of quiz nights, rock to live bands and, of course, enjoy a tasty pint or two.

If you enjoyed this book, you may also be interested in...

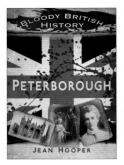

Bloody British History Peterborough

JEAN HOOPER

There is the darker side to Peterborough's history. All manner of incredible events have occurred in the city: Roman occupations; Saxon murders and miracles; riots and revolts; battles, diseases, disasters and plagues. Including more than sixty illustrations, and with the history of institutions such as the prisoner-of-war camps of the Napoleonic era and the slums and workhouses of the Victorian age, you'll never see the city in the same way again.

978 0 7524 8271 2

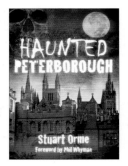

Haunted Peterborough

STUART ORME

Peterborough has a rich and fascinating history, stretching back 3,500 years to the Bronze Age. The city is a vibrant place dominated by its Norman cathedral. But the city has a sinister and spooky side too. This book explores many of the city's historic buildings and their ghost stories, including Peterborough Cathedral precincts. It also covers the spectres, stories and sightings at Peterborough Museum, one of Britain's most paranormally active buildings.

978 0 7524 7654 4

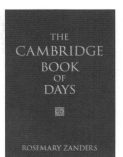

The Cambridge Book of Days

ROSEMARY ZANDERS

Taking you through the year day by day, *The Cambridge Book of Days* contains a quirky, eccentric, amusing or important event or fact from different periods of history, many of which had a major impact on the religious and political history of England as a whole. Ideal for dipping into, this addictive little book will keep you entertained and informed. Featuring hundreds of snippets of information gleaned from the vaults of Cambridge's archives, it will delight residents and visitors alike.

978 0 7524 5953 0

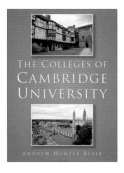

The Colleges of Cambridge University

ANDREW HUNTER BLAIR

This is not just 'another book about Cambridge'. It is unique in that it brings together in one publication the thirty-one colleges that comprise the University of Cambridge. Following a brief introduction and history of each college, there follows details of that college's unique features.Thoroughly researched and fully illustrated by the author with a wealth of stunning photographs, this book gives a unique insight into the workings, both past and present, of Cambridge University.

978 0 7524 7948 4

Visit our website and discover thousands of other History Press books.

www.thehistorypress.co.uk